Hands-On Ancient History

History and activities of the
Aztecs

Lisa Klobuchar

www.heinemann.co.uk/library
Visit our website to find out more information about Heinemann Library books.

To order:
☎ Phone 44 (0) 1865 888066
Send a fax to 44 (0) 1865 314091
Visit the Heinemann Bookshop at www.heinemann.co.uk/library to browse our
catalogue and order online.

First published in Great Britain by Heinemann Library, Halley Court, Jordan Hill, Oxford OX2 8EJ, part of Harcourt Education. Heinemann is a registered trademark of Harcourt Education Ltd.

Editorial: Audrey Stokes
Design: Kimberly R. Miracle in collaboration with Cavedweller Studio
Picture research: Mica Brancic
Production: Camilla Crask

Origination: Chroma Graphics
Printed and bound in China by WKT Company Limited

10-digit ISBN 0431080836
13-digit ISBN 9780431080833
11 10 09 08 07
10 9 8 7 6 5 4 3 2 1

British Library Cataloguing in Publication Data
Klobuchar, Lisa
Aztecs. – (Hands on ancient history)
1. Aztecs – Social life and customs – Juvenile literature
2. Aztecs – History – Juvenile literature
3. Mexico – Civilization – Juvenile literature
I. Title
972'.018
A full catalogue record for this book is available from the British Library.

Acknowledgements
The author and publishers are grateful to the following for permission to reproduce photographs: Alamy Images, pp. **15** (Mireille Vautier), **17** (Rob Bartee); Ancient Art and Architecture Collection, p. **7** (C M Dixon); Art Directors and Trip, pp. **8** (Helene Rogers), **16** (University Of Essex), **26** (The University of Essex); Art Resource NY, pp. **10** (Werner Forman), **12** (Werner Forman), **9** (SEF); Bridgeman Art Library, pp. **4** (Stapleton Collection), **18** (Private Collection, Boltin Picture Library); Corbis, pp. **5** (Bettmann), **11** (Gianni Dagli Orti), **13** (Kevin Schafer), **22** (Werner Forman); Harcourt, pp. **21** (David Rigg), **25** (David Rigg), **29** (David Rigg); Mexicolore, p. **14**.

Cover photographs of a man wearing a green Aztec headdress (foreground) reproduced with permission of Alamy Images (Felix Stensson) and the holy city of Teotihuacan (background) reproduced with permission of Getty Images.

The publishers would like to thank Julia Marchenko, Eric Utech and Kathy Peltan for their assistance in the preparation of this book.

Every effort has been made to contact copyright holders of any material reproduced in this book. Any omissions will be rectified in subsequent printings if notice is given to the publishers.

Contents

Chapter 1: Who were the Aztecs? 4

Chapter 2: Daily life 10

Chapter 3: Gossip and games 14

Chapter 4: Hands-on ancient history. 16

    Recipe: Corn tortillas 16

    Activity: Make a feather headdress 18

    Activity: Make a codex 22

    Activity: Make a *patolli* board 26

Glossary 30

More books to read 30

A note to teachers 31

Index. 32

Some words are shown in bold, **like this.** You can find out what they mean by looking in the glossary.

Chapter 1: Who were the Aztecs?

The **ancestors** of the Aztecs were **hunter-gatherers**. They roamed through the deserts. They wore hides and hunted with light bows and arrows.

In the 1200s, the ancestors of the Aztecs arrived at Lake Texcoco in the Valley of Mexico. They began to claim land. Finally, the Aztec ancestors started to fight with the people who lived there before them. The Aztecs beat the other groups and built the city of Tenochtitlán. The city was named after the ruler, Tenoch. Tenochtitlán became the capital of the Aztec **empire**.

By making war on neighbouring kingdoms, the Aztecs built an empire. During the 1400s and early 1500s, the Aztecs ruled a large area of central and southern Mexico. The empire reached its peak in the early 1500s, under the emperor Montezuma II.

In 1519, the Spanish explorer Hernan Cortés arrived. At first Montezuma welcomed

This picture shows the emperor Montezuma wearing traditional costume.

Timeline

1200s	1325	1502	1519	1521
Ancestors of Aztecs begin to settle in the Valley of Mexico, around Lake Texcoco	The city of Tenochtitlán is founded	Montezuma II becomes Aztec ruler	Spanish explorer Hernan Cortés arrives in the Valley of Mexico	Spanish conquer Aztec empire

him. He gave him gifts and held feasts. But he soon became worried because the Spaniards were joining with neighbouring kingdoms against the Aztecs. The Spaniards had better armour and weapons than the Aztecs. They were highly trained warriors.

When Montezuma heard that the Spanierds had joined his enemies, he knew his forces could not beat them in open battle. Montezuma decided his only choice was to invite the Spaniards into Tenochtitlán. But Cortés and his men tricked Montezuma and captured him. They kept Montezuma captive in his royal apartments. Other leaders and Aztec warriors attacked the Spaniards in Montezuma's palace. No one knows exactly how it happened, but Montezuma was killed at this time.

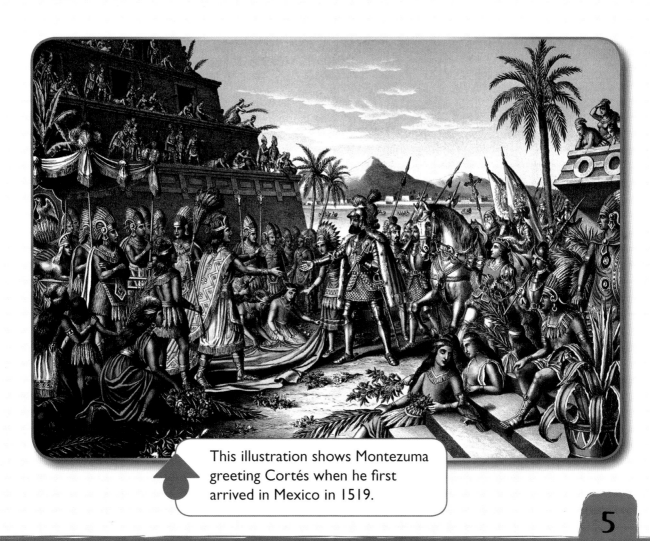

This illustration shows Montezuma greeting Cortés when he first arrived in Mexico in 1519.

A battle was fought in Tenochtitlán. The Spaniards escaped from the city at night. They attacked again in April 1521. The Aztecs fought hard, but many died in the fighting. They also died of starvation, lack of water, and disease. In August 1521, the last Aztec emperor was captured. The Aztecs were forced to give up.

Within ten years the **empire** was ruled by Spain. The Spanish **converted** the surviving Aztecs to Christianity. They also made many of the Aztecs slaves.

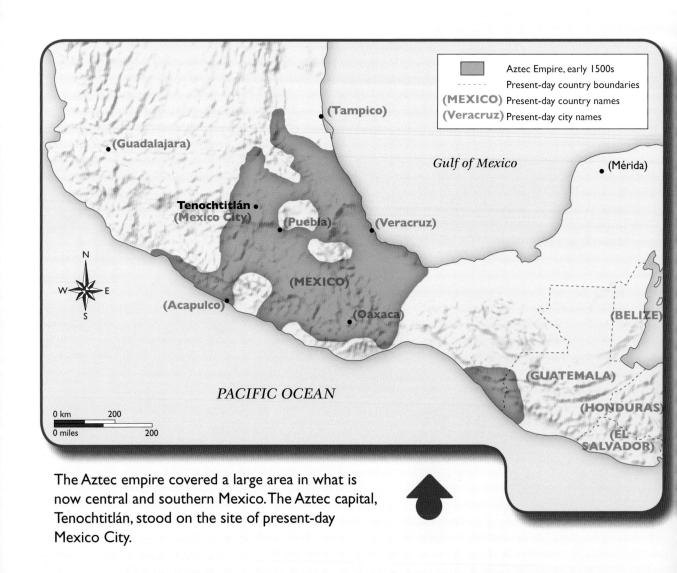

The Aztec empire covered a large area in what is now central and southern Mexico. The Aztec capital, Tenochtitlán, stood on the site of present-day Mexico City.

Aztec art

For the Aztecs, art was connected to religion and nature. The most highly prized Aztec artists were painters. Painters created the codices, or books, that recorded all the important parts of Aztec life. Aztec painters also used their skills to decorate pottery.

Aztec artists created beautiful works of art using feathers that they collected from colourful birds such as parrots and hummingbirds. They made headdresses, shields, cloaks, fans, and clothing for rulers, warriors, and other people. Feather work was so respected that even Aztecs of the upper classes worked hard to master the craft. Aztecs admired feather work even more than goldsmithing. Gold was used to make jewellery, cups, jars, masks, and other objects.

Aztecs were master goldsmiths. This gold pendant shows an Aztec ruler dressed for a ritual. He holds a battle axe, a staff shaped like a snake, and a shield.

Aztec religion

Religion and **spiritual** beliefs were at the centre of Aztec life. Aztecs believed that all parts of nature, from birds to ears of corn, and even rocks and wind, were alive with spirit. Even works of art had spiritual meaning. The Sun Stone is a famous stone carving. It shows the Aztecs' view of how the world was created.

Aztecs believed that a god named Ometecuhtli, or Two Lord, and a goddess named Omecihuatl, or Two Lady, created the world. They had four sons. Each of these sons ruled over one direction – east, west, north, and south. The gods tore apart a terrifying she-monster. Out of her body came plants, rivers, valleys, and mountains. But in exchange for these gifts, she demanded human blood. The Aztec religion had many rituals that included the spilling of blood.

The Sun Stone shows the Aztecs' beliefs about the history of the world. They believed that the Earth had been created and destroyed four times and that they lived in the fifth era.

The Aztecs also worshipped a rain god, a goddess of water, fire and earth gods, plant gods, a sun god, and many others. They believed that the gods gave them life, created the world, and provided all the things the people needed to live. The power of the gods showed itself in powerful natural events such as thunder, wind, rain, and rushing rivers.

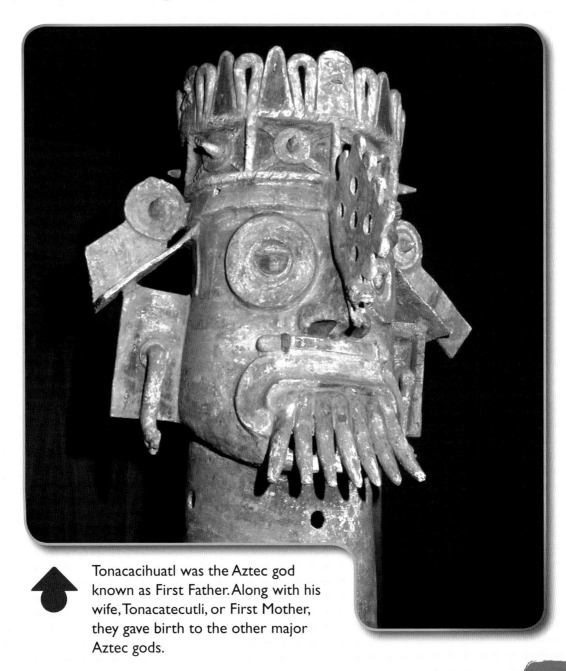

Tonacacihuatl was the Aztec god known as First Father. Along with his wife, Tonacatecutli, or First Mother, they gave birth to the other major Aztec gods.

Chapter 2: Daily life

The Aztecs believed that every person had a place in society. Their society was divided according to rank. Some people had more power, money, and rights than others. Nobles were at the top of the Aztec social scale. Land-owning commoners were in the middle. At the bottom were farmers who worked the land of others, and slaves.

Nobles owned most of the land. They worked as warriors, clerks, judges, historians, and tax collectors. All the nobles received tribute, or payments in goods and services, from the commoners. Boys and girls of the noble class had their own schools. There they learned subjects they would need to take their place as leaders at the top of society when they grew up.

This pendant would have been worn by a nobleman or high-priest. It is made from jade.

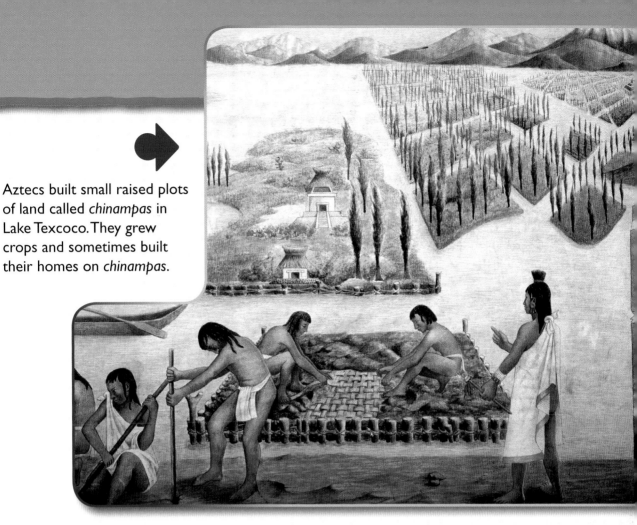

Aztecs built small raised plots of land called *chinampas* in Lake Texcoco. They grew crops and sometimes built their homes on *chinampas*.

Some commoners owned small plots of land where they grew crops. Some of them fished for a living. Others ran small businesses. Still others did hard, physical work, such as building and repairing palaces and public buildings. Commoners could improve themselves by becoming skilled artists, merchants, or warriors. Children of commoners also went to school. They mostly learned work skills, the basics of warfare, and how to be a good citizen.

In times of hardship, a person or a whole family could sell themselves into slavery. Thieves and people in debt or gamblers who lost all their money might become slaves for a time. Owners did not pay slaves for their work. However, slaves were allowed to own property and were free to marry whoever they wished. Slaves could make money in their spare time, and some even became rich. If a slave became rich enough, he or she could buy his or her freedom.

Home life

Aztecs saw themselves as belonging to their town or city, then their community, and finally their family. Daily life centred around the local community. In most localities, people of all classes and jobs mingled. Each area had its own special god or goddess and a **temple** dedicated to it. People of the local community gathered at the temple to worship.

Aztecs lived in single-family homes. A family was made up of a husband and wife and their children. Women took care of the house, and men worked outside the home. Children stayed with their parents until they married, around the age of 15 for women and 20 for men. Children were raised with strict discipline. Adults might prick misbehaving children with thorns.

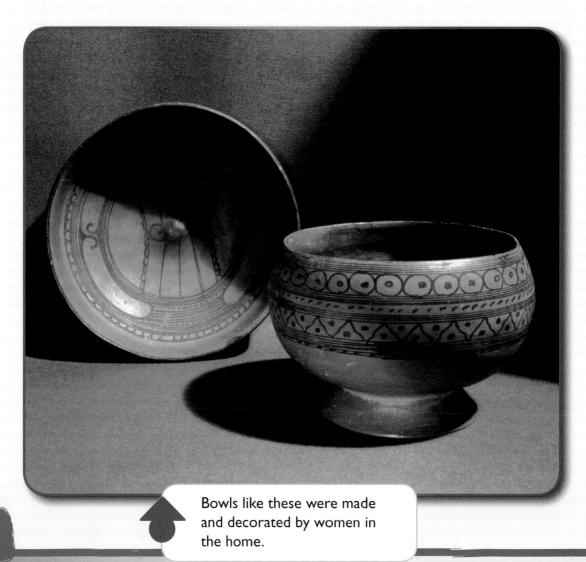

Bowls like these were made and decorated by women in the home.

Popcorn, peanuts, and lizards

The main food of the Aztecs was corn. They made corn flatbread called tortillas, as well as corn cakes and porridge. The Aztecs ate many types of beans, grains, vegetables, and fruits. Fish and meat were eaten in smaller amounts. Aztecs ate lizards, insects, and worms, too. They also enjoyed popcorn and peanuts.

Chocolate and chilli

Chocolate is made from the beans of cacao trees. These trees grew in the Valley of Mexico. The Aztecs used cacao beans to make a chocolate drink. Only the upper classes could drink chocolate because it was scarce. The drink was made by roasting and grinding cacao beans. Then the cacoa powder was mixed with water. The Aztecs beat the liquid with a wooden whisk and flavoured it with vanilla and chilli powder.

The prickly pear cactus was one source of food for the Aztecs.

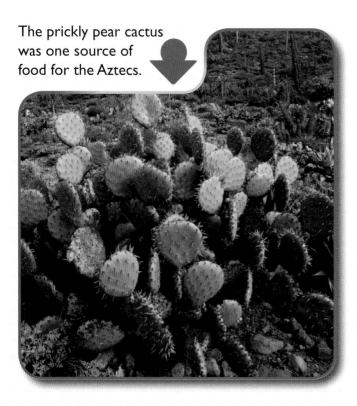

13

Chapter 3: Gossip and games

Every Aztec community had a market. The market was an important social centre. Officials patrolled them to make sure all business was carried out honestly. People of all ages flocked to the market places. Buying and selling was fun. It was also a place to meet and gossip with friends.

Aztec children were expected to work hard, study hard, and behave properly from a young age. Much of their time was spent learning the skills they would need as adults. But they had some time for play. Many of their toys were smaller versions of grown-up tools. Boys played with weapons, for example, and girls played with spinning and cooking utensils.

Aztec children played with toys like this pottery dog. They pulled it along on wheels.

Aztecs played *ollama* on an I-shaped ball court called a *tlachtli*. The object of the game was to use the elbows, knees, and hips to move a hard rubber ball through a stone ring.

Aztec athletes played a game called *ollama*. It was similar to football and basketball, but much rougher. *Ollama* was played on a ball court called a *tlachtli*, which was shaped like a capital letter I. High up on each side of the upright part of the 'I' was a stone ring. The object of the game was to get a hard rubber ball through the ring. Players could use only their elbows, knees, and hips to move the ball.

Another popular form of entertainment was playing a board game called *patolli*. *Patolli* was similar to backgammon. Players raced to be the first to move their game pieces around a board.

Chapter 4: Hands-on ancient history

By doing the hands-on activities and crafts in this chapter, you will get a feel for what life was like for the Aztecs.

Recipe: Corn tortillas

Corn was the most important part of the Aztecs' diet. The most common item made from corn was tortillas. After you make your corn tortillas, use them to scoop up beans, or wrap them around cheese, meat, or vegetables, or any combination of these foods. Aztecs prepared corn for making tortillas by cooking corn kernels with lime to make a dough. They ground the dough on a flat piece of stone. Then they used their hands to form flat, round tortillas, just like those many people enjoy today.

Supplies and ingredients
- mixing bowl
- large frying pan, or griddle
- spatula
- 300 g corn meal, (also called masa)
- cooking oil or non-stick spray

This picture from a codex shows Aztecs eating a meal together.

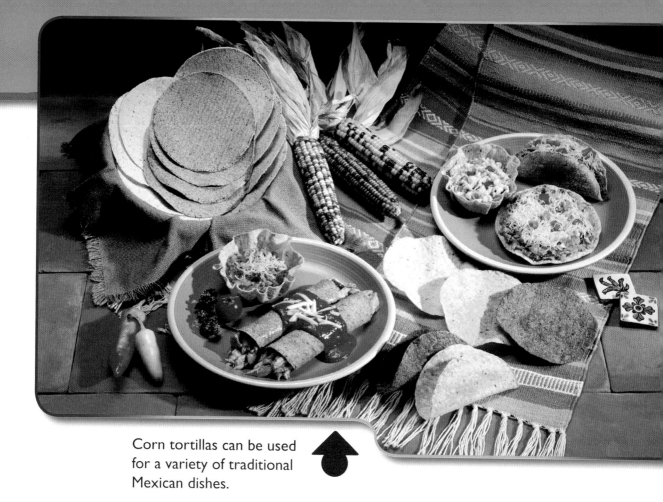

Corn tortillas can be used for a variety of traditional Mexican dishes.

1 Follow the directions on the corn flour package to create dough.

2 After making the dough, allow it to sit for five minutes. This makes the dough easier to handle.

3 Form a ball of dough about 2.5 centimetres in diameter.

4 Sprinkle flour on your hands to prevent sticking. Pat the ball back and forth between your hands. Pat it until it is flat and thin.

5 Coat the pan lightly with cooking oil or non-stick spray. Heat the pan on medium-high heat.

6 Place the tortilla on the pan and cook until slightly brown. Flip the tortilla with the spatula. It should take about two minutes to cook the tortilla.

7 You can serve the tortillas with cheese, beans, vegetables, or meat.

Activity: Make a feather headdress

Feather work was among the most highly prized Aztec art. Aztecs raised birds for their feathers. Hunters also caught birds in the forests. Feather workers might tie the shafts, or bare ends, of the feathers into cloth while it was being woven. Or they glued or tied feathers to a base of cotton or a stiff leaf. Warriors, priests, nobles, and rulers wore feather ornaments and clothing at important ceremonies and festivals. Commoners were not allowed to wear feather items.

Warning!

Make sure you read all of the directions before beginning the project.

Feather work was very important to the Aztecs. You should treat your headdress with dignity and respect.

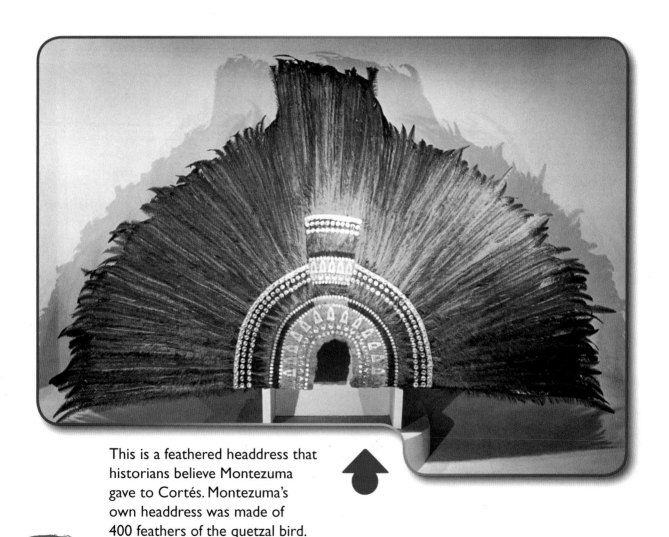

This is a feathered headdress that historians believe Montezuma gave to Cortés. Montezuma's own headdress was made of 400 feathers of the quetzal bird.

Supplies

- thin card or stiff paper cut to 60 cm by 5 cm. (option: use craft leather available at craft shops, cut to size.)
- pencil
- scissors
- stapler or sticky tape
- glue
- sequins, glitter, foil
- feathers (available at craft shops) or coloured paper cut into feather shapes
- crayons or markers

❶ Your thin card or stiff paper will be the headband. Use a pencil to create a design or pattern on your card or paper. This could be shapes and lines, or an illustration of a story. For example, you could illustrate various animals or gods that were important to the Aztecs, such as jaguars or the feathered serpent.

❷ Use crayons or markers to colour your design or illustration. You can also glue sequins, glitter, or foil onto the headband.

❸ Glue, staple, or tape the feathers onto the back of the headband so they poke out along the top. Make a pattern from different colours or shapes of feathers. (See Picture A)

A

4 Ask someone to wrap the headband around your head so the two ends overlap at the back of your head. Ask them to use a pencil to mark the spot on the headband where one end overlaps the other. (See Picture B)

B

C

5 Take the headband off your head and overlap the ends so that they match the mark that was made. Use sticky tape or a stapler to fasten the headband on the inside, so it stays in a circle. (See Picture C)

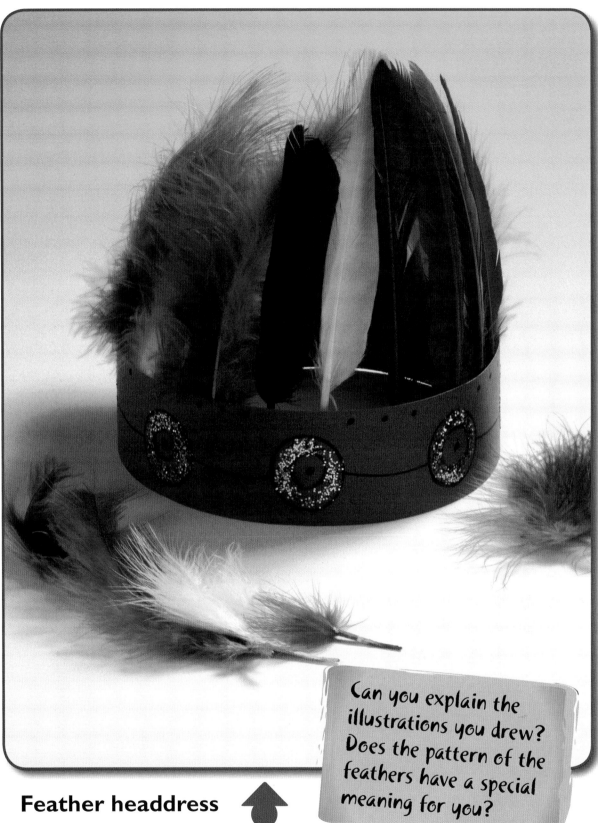

Can you explain the illustrations you drew? Does the pattern of the feathers have a special meaning for you?

Feather headdress

You can make your feather headdress in any combination of colours.

Activity: make a codex

Aztec artists recorded important information about their world and their beliefs in codices. Codices were kept by wise teachers called *tlamatinime,* or "knowers of things". The illustrations in the codices look a little like cartoons. They show pictures of gods and goddesses, animals, and symbols representing calendar points and points in the sky. The codices were made from the bark of the fig tree, or from animal hide. They were folded back and forth, like a fan.

Supplies

- one piece of 15 cm by 45 cm drawing or coloured paper, or other long paper
- 2 pieces of stiff, coloured card, between ½ and 1 cm taller and wider than the paper above
- 60 cm of coloured string or wool
- glue

This illustration from the Codex Cospi shows the planet Venus attacking warriors.

1 Place the paper in front of you, horizontally.

2 Fold it in half down the middle. (See Picture A)

3 Fold the top page in half by folding it back to meet the first fold. (See Picture B)

4 Turn the paper over and repeat this process, folding the top page back to meet the first fold.

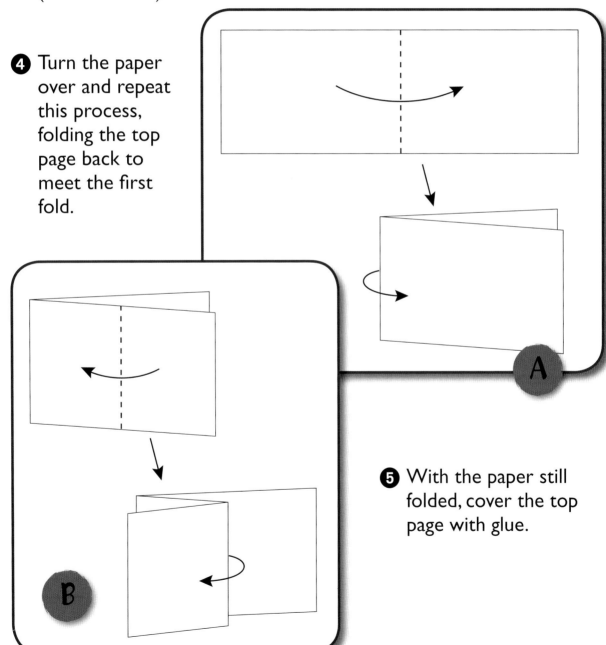

5 With the paper still folded, cover the top page with glue.

6 Place one piece of card for the cover face down in front of you. Carefully pick up the folded bunch of paper, and glue the top page down to the card. Make sure it is centred and even. (See Picture C)

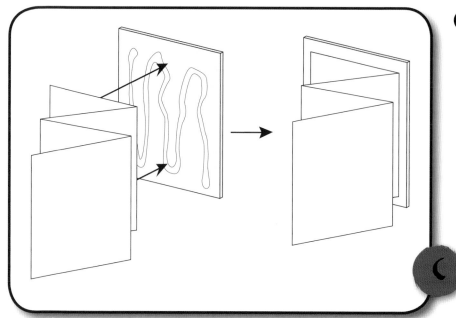

7 Now, with the last page of the folded paper facing up, cover it with glue.

8 Repeat the process of placing the other piece of card in front of you, and carefully gluing the last page down to it. Check again to make sure it lines up with the other card cover.

9 Put the string or wool across the back of the book, from side to side. Make sure that the ends of the string or wool are even.

10 Wrap the string or wool around the book and tie it across the front in a bow.

11 Turn the book back over and glue the string or wool in place. (See Picture D)

GLUE

D

⑫ When you want to write in your book, untie the string and put the book down on its back.

Will you use the codex for drawings or words?

Codex

This codex is ready for words and drawings.

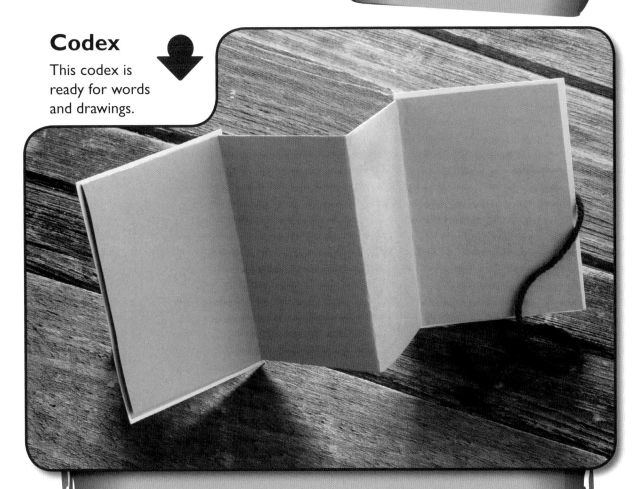

FOR MORE PAGES IN YOUR BOOK

Before adding the back cover, take a second piece of long paper and fold it just as you did with the first one. Glue this set of pages to the last page in your first set. Then glue the back cover to the last page of the second set. You can also make more pages by making each one smaller. Instead of folding the long paper in half, try folding it into thirds, then folding each third in half.

Activity: Make a *patolli* board

A *patolli* board was like a big X divided into squares. The players threw beans that worked like dice. The winner was the player who was the first to move his or her six pebbles from the beginning to the end of the board. The game often drew crowds of spectators, People would bet on the outcome. They could win or lose valuable goods. In fact, there are records of people losing everything they owned on *patolli* games and having to sell themselves into slavery.

Warning!

Make sure you read all the directions before beginning the project.

Aztecs played *patolli* on an X-shaped board.

Supplies
- thin card or large drawing paper, about 60 cm by 90 cm
- pencil
- drawing paper or coloured paper (optional)
- ruler or long measuring stick
- marker pens, crayons, or paint
- 7 dried beans or 1 dice and 2 playing pieces

1. Use a pencil to draw a large "X" or cross shape on the card. Make it big – each arm of the "X" or cross should be about 5 or 7.5 cm wide, and long enough to reach almost from one end of the card to the other. Use a ruler or measuring stick to make straight lines. This is your *patolli* game board.

A

2. There are four arms to the *patolli* board. Draw lines across the arms where they meet in the middle. This will make a box in the middle. (See Picture A)

3. Draw across each arm of the *patolli* board so that you divide each arm into three equal sections. (See Picture B)

B

4. Draw a line from the box in the centre down the middle of each arm to its end. You'll be drawing four lines in all. (See Picture C)

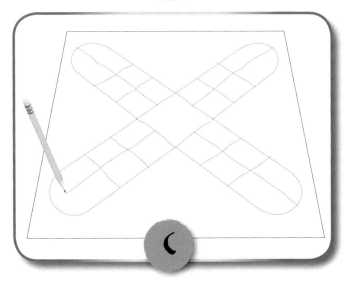

5 Now each arm has six sections. Look at the box in the middle of the *patolli* board. Draw a line from one corner of the box to the opposite corner. Repeat this so that you have drawn an "X" in the box.

6 The "X" that you just made divides the box into four triangles. Each triangle is now the seventh section of each arm of the *patolli* board.

7 Make a blue circle in the end section of one arm. Make a blue crown at the end of the opposite arm. (See Picture D)

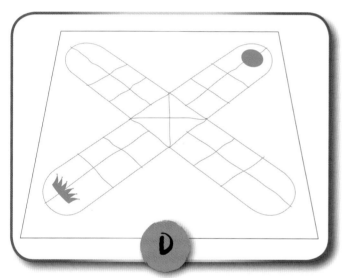

8 Repeat this process so there is a green circle and a green crown at the ends of the last arm.

9 Pick 8 empty sections on the *patolli* board at random. Draw jaguar heads in each. Pick another 8 empty sections and draw 8 marigold flowers. You can draw the jaguars and marigolds on different paper, cut them out, and glue them on the *patolli* board. You could even cut out pictures of jaguars and marigolds from magazines.

10 Use 2 dried beans to make playing pieces or markers. Use paint or pens to colour one of the beans blue, and the other one green.

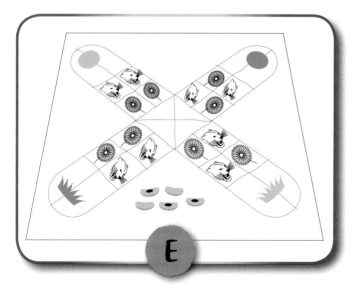

11 Make a dot on each of your remaining 5 beans. The beans serve as your dice. When you throw the beans, count how many land with a dot showing. This will tell you how many spaces to move when you play *patolli*. (See Picture E)

How to play

Start each game piece on the circle of the same colour. The goal is to move your piece down the board to the crown of the same colour, and back to the beginning. Roll the beans or dice to find out how many spaces to move when it's your turn. If you land on a jaguar, you lose a turn. If you land on a marigold, you get an extra turn.

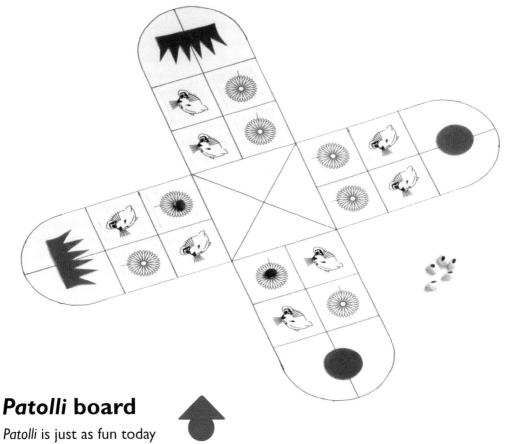

Patolli board

Patolli is just as fun today as it was 500 years ago.

What other decorations can you add to your game board?

Glossary

ancestor person who is a relative from an earlier time. For example, grandparents, great-grandparents, and great-great-grandparents are ancestors.

convert to change a person from one set of beliefs to another, sometimes by force

empire group of countries ruled by a single country or ruler

hunter-gatherer person who gets food by hunting animals and collecting foods such as fruits, roots, plants, nuts, and other things that grow naturally

spiritual things that have to do with people's souls rather than their bodies

temple place where holy objects are kept and where people go to pray

More books to read

Arts and Crafts of the Ancient World: Aztecs and Maya, Ting Morris (Watts Publishing, 2006)

Craft Topics: The Aztecs, Ruth Thomson (Sea to Sea Publications, 2004)

Excavating the Past: The Aztec Empire, Tony Allan (Heinemann Library, 2004)

History Opens Windows: The Aztecs, Jane Shuter (Heinemann Library, 2006)

Understanding People in the Past: The Aztecs, Rosemary Rees (Heinemann Library, 2006)

The instructions for the crafts and activities are designed to allow pupils to work as independently as possible. However, it is always a good idea to make a prototype before assigning any project so that pupils can see how their own work will look when completed. Prior to introducing these activities, teachers should collect and prepare the materials and be ready for any modifications that may be necessary. Participating in the project-making process will help teachers understand the directions and be ready to assist pupils with difficult steps. Teachers might also choose to adapt or modify the projects to better suit the needs of an individual child or class. No one knows the levels of achievement pupils will reach better than their teacher.

While it is preferable for pupils to work as independently as possible, there is some flexibility in regards to project materials and tools. They can vary according to what is available. For instance, while standard white glue may be most familiar, there might be times when a teacher will choose to speed up a project by using a hot glue gun to join materials. Where plaster gauze is not availabe, papier mâché can often be used. Likewise, while a project may call for leather cord, in most instances it is possible to substitute plastic rope or even wool or string. Acrylic paint may be recommended because it adheres better to a material like felt or plastic, but other types of paint would be suitable as well. Circles can be drawn with a compass, or simply by tracing a cup, roll of tape, or other circular object. Allowing pupils a broad spectrum of creativity and opportunities to problem-solve within the parameters of a given project will encourage their critical thinking skills most fully.

Each project contains a question within the directions. These questions are meant to be thought-provoking and promote discussion while pupils work on the project.

Index

art 7

ball courts 14, 15

cacao beans 13
children 10, 11, 12, 14,
   15
chinampas 11
chocolate 13
Christianity 6
codex (activity) 22–25
codices 7, 22
commoners 10, 11, 18
corn 13, 16
corn tortillas (recipe)
   16–17
Cortés, Hernan 4, 5,
   18
creation story 8, 9

discipline 12

empire 4

families 12
farming 10, 11
feather headdress
   (activity) 18–21
feather work 7, 18
festivals 18
food 13, 16–17
games 14–15, 26–29

gods and goddesses
   8–9, 12, 22
goldsmithing 7

homes 12
human sacrifices 8
hunter-gatherers 4

Lake Texcoco 4, 11

markets 14
marriage 11, 12
Montezuma II 4–5, 18

neighbourhoods 12
nobles 7, 10, 13, 18

ollama 14–15

patolli 15, 26
patolli board
   (activity) 26–29
poetry 7
pottery 7
prickly pear cactus 13

quetzal bird 18

religion 7, 8–9, 12
riddles 7

schools 10, 11

slaves 6, 10, 11, 26
society 10
Spaniards 4–6
Sun Stone 8

teachers 22
temples 12
Tenochtitlán 4, 5, 6
Tonacacihuatl 9
toys 14, 15
tribute 10

warriors 10, 11, 18
women and girls 12,
   14
work 10, 11

Titles in the *Hands on Ancient History* series include:

Hardback   978 0 431 08083 3

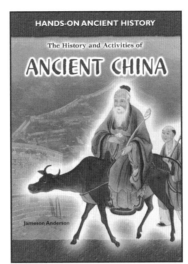

Hardback   978 0 431 08086 4

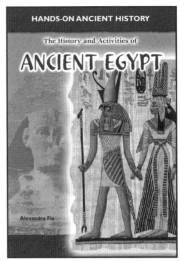

Hardback   978 0 431 08084 0

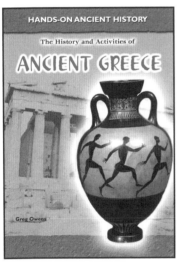

Hardback   978 0 431 08085 7

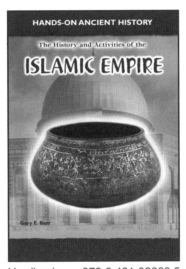

Hardback   978 0 431 08089 5

Hardback   978 0 431 08087 1

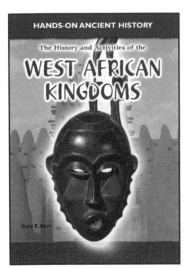

Hardback   978 0 431 08088 8

Find out about other titles from Heinemann Library on our website www.heinemann.co.uk/library